AMERICAN BOY

⸙ THE ADVENTURES OF MARK TWAIN ⸙

written and illustrated by **DON BROWN**

HOUGHTON MIFFLIN COMPANY

BOSTON 2003

FOR NANCY AND CHRIS

The text of this book is set in ITC Century Book.
The illustrations are pen and ink and watercolor on paper.

Library of Congress Cataloging-in-Publication Data

Brown, Don.
American boy : the adventures of Mark Twain / written and illustrated
by Don Brown.
p. cm.
Summary: Provides a brief biography of the noted American writer who was born Samuel Clemens.
Includes bibliographical references (p.   )
ISBN 0-618-17997-6
1. Twain, Mark, 1835–1910—Childhood and youth—Juvenile literature.
2. Authors, American—19th century—Biography—Juvenile literature.
[1. Twain, Mark, 1835–1910. 2. Authors, American.] I. Title.
PS1332 .B76 2003
818'.409—dc21

2002151177

Manufactured in the United States of America
WOZ 10 9 8 7 6 5 4 3 2 1

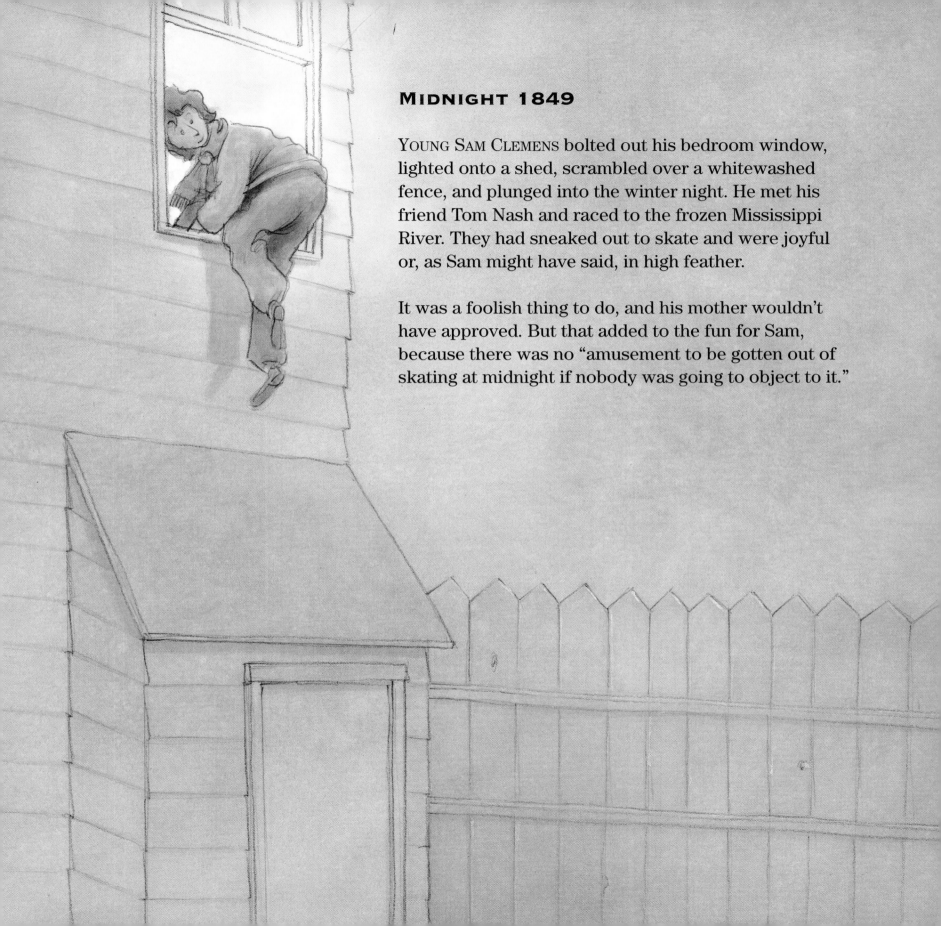

MIDNIGHT 1849

Young Sam Clemens bolted out his bedroom window, lighted onto a shed, scrambled over a whitewashed fence, and plunged into the winter night. He met his friend Tom Nash and raced to the frozen Mississippi River. They had sneaked out to skate and were joyful or, as Sam might have said, in high feather.

It was a foolish thing to do, and his mother wouldn't have approved. But that added to the fun for Sam, because there was no "amusement to be gotten out of skating at midnight if nobody was going to object to it."

Sam and Tom had skated a half-mile out on the moonlit river when they suddenly heard grinding and rumbling. The ice was breaking up! The boys sped toward the shore, skipping from ice cake to ice cake on the frigid, open water.

"We flew along at full speed whenever the moonlight sifting down between the clouds enabled us to tell which was ice and which was water," Sam later recalled.

Tom spilled into the river. Though he managed to reach the shore, the dunking proved dear for him. Tom later took ill, and the fever robbed him of his hearing for life.

Meanwhile, Sam returned home dry and safe, and with a great tale to boot.

Sam loved a great tale.

In time, he would write some of America's greatest tales.

"I COULD SEE NO PROMISE IN HIM," Sam's mother, Jane, said of him on his birth in Missouri on November 30, 1835.

He was small and weak, and the excitement of his arrival was nearly undone by the fear of his quick departure. Still, Jane was hopeful. Surely the appearance of Halley's comet, burning bright in the sky, was a good omen. Halley's comet or not, Sam survived.

In 1839, the Clemens family moved to Hannibal, Missouri, a drowsy patchwork of simple streets, shops, houses, yards, and alleys beside the Mississippi River where, on a summer morning, roaming pigs might appear to outnumber the people.

Sam's father, John, had great expectations of success in Hannibal. But the stern, unsmiling man had no talent for business, and the family's fortune tumbled instead.

Despite the poverty, Sam's mother maintained a "sunshiney disposition."

She also could be wickedly funny, told a good story, and had a weakness for animals; one time, she provided shelter to nineteen cats. Sam was very much like his mother.

He was also a dreamer and a prankster. Hannibal proved to be a paradise in which Sam could exercise his enormous imagination and taste for mischief. The town brimmed with like-minded boys. Will Bowen was Sam's best friend. The two jumped at the chance for monkey business.

They played hooky,

sneaked from their beds to explore sleeping Hannibal

and once loosened a giant boulder, sending it crashing down a hill and into a shed.

Both Sam and Will kept a frowned-upon friendship with Hannibal's wild boy, Tom Blankenship.

Tom was from a seedy family and was dreaded by the town's respectable mothers. He never went to school or church, nor need obey anybody. Sam ignored Tom's outcast reputation.

"He was ignorant, unwashed, and insufficiently fed; but he had as good a heart as any boy had," Sam said.

SAM

WILL

TOM BLANKENSHIP

Sam, Tom, Will, and others roamed the forests, acting out the stories of knights, pirates, or highwaymen that Sam discovered in the books he loved so much. *Robin Hood* was one of their favorites, and the boys would "rather be outlaws for one year in Sherwood Forest than President of the United States forever."

Sam and his gang explored McDowell's Cave, a warren of dark, crooked passageways that "ran into each other and out again and led nowhere." It was a spooky place of swooping bats and a dead body—a teenage girl who had been placed there, instead of in a cemetery, by her eccentric father. The boys were convinced the cave was haunted.

Like the other boys, young Sam was certain there *were* ghosts. He believed in spells, too. And potions. And in the magic of spunk water, rainwater left in rotten tree stumps. A dead rat on a string was a powerful charm, one worth offering to his sweet-heart, Laura Hawkins.

The wild forests and the creepy cave were grand, but the Mississippi River, "the majestic, magnificent Mississippi, rolling its mile-wide tide along," beat everything.

With their paddlewheels churning, steamboats plowed their way up and down the river, hauling goods and people. The arrival of a steamboat electrified Sam, electrified *everyone*.

S-t-e-a-m-boat a-comin'! The call would come, and the boat, a great gaudy thing, would glide up to the wharf, wreathed in smoke and steam. Once landed, passengers and freight came and went in a hubbub. When the boat departed, the boat's leadsman tested the water's depth and shouted the measurements to the captain; the boat needed to be steered into deep water or risk running aground.

"Quarter twain!"

"Half twain!"

"Mark twain!"

Mark twain meant deep, safe water.

Sam fished the Mississippi, rafted it, skated it, and collected turtle eggs along its banks. And he swam it . . . once he learned how. Sam later claimed he "drowned" nine times before he learned to swim.

One such time was in Bear Creek, a finger of water that fed the Mississippi. Sam spilled from the log he was riding and slipped beneath the surface. Luckily, a slave woman saw Sam's fingers above the water, seized them, and pulled Sam out.

Like the river, slavery was a fixture of Sam's life.

"In my boyhood days, I was not aware there was anything wrong about it. The local papers said nothing against it; the local pulpit taught us God approved it," he said.

Still, Sam sensed that slavery was a woeful thing. Once, he witnessed a dozen chained slaves waiting to be shipped down the river.

"Those were the saddest faces I have ever seen," he said.

Of the black boys and girls he met while wandering Hannibal, Sam said, "We were comrades and yet not comrades. Color and condition . . . rendered complete fusion impossible."

Sam did find a "good friend, ally, and advisor" in Uncle Dan'l, a slave owned by Sam's uncle. Uncle Dan'l was a teller of tall tales and ghost stories, and Sam, a lover of tales and stories, was drawn to the warm-hearted man.

"I can see the white and black children grouped on the hearth, with the firelight playing on their faces . . . and I can hear Uncle Dan'l telling the immortal tales," Sam would later recall.

Sam's father died in 1847, and the Clemens family drifted into deeper poverty. Sam found odd jobs to earn money. When he was about fifteen years old, he quit school, apprenticed to a printer, and learned to set type.

Before an article could be printed, each metal letter had to be plucked, one at a time, from a case and arranged in lines called sticks. The sticks needed to be assembled in trays, which were then inked and printed. Sam came to appreciate writing as something more than scribbling—it was constructed letter by letter, word by word, sentence by sentence.

Sam's older brother Orion started a newspaper, and there Sam not only set type and printed pages, but also wrote stories: news and gossip and silly things, part real, part invented, that offended some people and amused others.

"My literature attracted the town's attention, but not its admiration," Sam said.

But Orion's newspaper and Hannibal began to seem small and cramped. Sam craved something else, anything else. He became "wild with impatience to move-move-MOVE!"

So seventeen-year-old Samuel Clemens packed his bags, bid his mother farewell, and lit out. Hannibal would be his home nevermore.

FEBRUARY 1863

IN THE YEARS AFTERWARD, Sam was a riverboat pilot, a failed Confederate soldier, and an unsuccessful silver prospector. In Nevada, Sam drifted back into the newspaper business as a reporter.

At that time, writers sometimes used a "pen name," a name other than their own, to affix to their work. On February 3, 1863, Sam, recalling his Mississippi days, signed one of his dispatches "Mark Twain."

Sam must have felt it fit nicely, for he kept it. As Mark Twain, Sam traveled the world, wrote about it, and got rich. The lover of great stories became the writer of great stories. He lectured, met presidents and kings, and became famous.

Bye and bye, he remembered his boyhood, the glad morning of his life. As if skating ice cakes on a frozen river, Sam skipped from memory to memory and wove together great tales, *The Adventures of Tom Sawyer* and *The Adventures of Huckleberry Finn*.

It was all there: Hannibal, the cave, the river—the magnificent river!—and, of course, the people of Sam's boyhood.

Sam was Tom Sawyer, at least part of him, because a bit of Will Bowen was Tom Sawyer, too. Tom Blankenship became Huck Finn. Sweetheart Laura Hawkins was in the books as Becky Thatcher. And a part of Uncle Dan'l was there as the big-hearted slave, Jim.

The books were read everywhere. They delighted most people, offended others, and made everyone think.

They still do.

Sam Clemens

Mark Twain

NOTE

ALTHOUGH SAMUEL LANGHORNE CLEMENS WAS BORN IN 1835, his more famous alter ego, Mark Twain, didn't come to life until 1863, when the irrepressibly imaginative Clemens conjured him up. Up until then, young Clemens had known only a knockabout life. His childhood was poverty-stricken, and his subsequent experiences as printer, riverboat pilot, Confederate soldier, prospector, and newspaperman were marked by only spotty success. It was while working as a reporter in Nevada that Clemens donned the Mark Twain persona. The pretense subsequently proved to be a remarkably good fit; as Twain, he found worldwide recognition as a short story writer, travel writer, lecturer, and novelist.

The Celebrated Jumping Frog of Calaveras County, Life on the Mississippi, Innocents Abroad, Roughing It, The Prince and the Pauper, and The Adventures of Tom Sawyer have found their way into America's literary canon, but it is The Adventures of Huckleberry Finn that is Twain's masterpiece and fuels the contention that Mark Twain is America's greatest writer. Even today, the book retains the power to spark heated arguments about race in America and regularly appears on lists of banned library books.

Sam Clemens died in 1910, his death coinciding, as did his birth, with the appearance of Halley's comet.

BIBLIOGRAPHY

Hoffman, Andrew. *Inventing Mark Twain.* New York: William Morrow, 1997.

Powers, Ron. *Dangerous Water.* New York: Basic Books, 1999.

Sanborn, Margaret. *Mark Twain: The Bachelor Years.* New York: Doubleday Dell, 1990.

Twain, Mark. *The Autobiography of Mark Twain.* Edited by Charles Neider. New York: Harper and Row, 1959.

———. *Hannibal, Huck, and Tom.* Edited by Walter Blair. Berkeley: University of California Press, 1969.

Ward, Geoffrey, and Dayton Duncan. *Mark Twain.* New York: Knopf, 2001.